Things I've Picked Up and Brought Home

Joyce Rachelle

Presentation by *BookLeaf Publishing*

Web: www.bookleafpub.com

E-mail: info@bookleafpub.com

ISBN: 9789357214551

First edition 2023

To anyone who has ever given me anything,

*even the stranger who unknowingly gave me
Covid-19.*

PREFACE

I'm not a big fan of introductions and I don't think I've ever written one before, but this, I think, is necessary.

I was coming home from work after a long, hard day and I hadn't even got out of my uniform yet when I decided for some reason to sign up for a 21-day poetry writing challenge. Goodness knows I had enough on my plate already, but my mind somehow thought that this was worth making time for. So here we are.

Poems usually come to me whenever they like, and it very often takes years for me to pack them into something substantial enough to call a book — the last one took me a decade to write — but this collection is the first of its kind, for me at least. A poem a day for twenty-one days turned out to be the therapy I didn't know I needed.

And in the following pages I share the transcript.

The Mug That Says 'Her Ladyship'

The mug that says 'Her Ladyship'
is sitting on my desk.
I wish that I could say someone
got it for me, but no,
I bought this one myself.

My mother used to say to me
when I was growing up
that I was the prettiest girl
in the world, that is,
equally as pretty
and as smart and as clever
as my two other sisters.

We believed her.

My aunt used to warn her friends
before they first met us,
never to say that her sister's
kids were ugly
or else my mum would
eat them alive.

We were perfect little
princesses, my mother told us so.

But now I sink into a chair
after a long day's slavish work,
dark crescents under my eyes
and my hair all out of place.
My boss had told me I was awful
and my friends hadn't backed me up
when I needed them.

I've come out mangled and deflated
from the bus I was thrown under,
I can barely stand on my feet.
My hands are shaking and the
mirror isn't kind.
I might as well be blind.

I might as well give in
to this paralysing blow,
but this mug is for Her Ladyship
and my mother told me so.

Vera

She was only little when we met,
and I was afraid I might kill her.
But I was hers and she was mine
and we were stuck with each other
whether we liked it or not
because those are the rules
for birthday presents.

I was told she liked tea now and then.
No, I've never made her a cup
and I haven't sung songs
or played Mozart for her benefit.
But she wanted for nothing, as I
gave her all I could give
while looking after myself,
so that I too could live.

While I searched for the music
I seemed to have traded for
the thing that you use to buy food.
While I searched for the voice
I seemed to have traded for
slivers of silence and solitude.
And the fresh cup of tea that I
skipped everyday just because there

was not enough time.
I had lost everything
that I used to call mine.

Then I woke up one morning, not
realising that Vera had grown
so much taller and bigger than
we last saw each other that first
time we got introduced.
Reaching far beyond her small space,
each day just a little bit more,
needing room enough to be.
How did I not see?

For all my distant, meagre care I
should have clearly known
I could not kill a creature with such
big dreams of her own.
Dreams that thrived on neglect
and cramped spaces,
unwilling to stay in unbearable
stasis.
If we didn't live in a cage we
wouldn't fight to be free.
I was staring at Vera who was
staring at me.

But enough now of this talk of
cages and spaces,

procrastination can take such
varied forms and faces.
All I'm really saying is
I'm done leaving it till tomorrow.
It's time I roll my sleeves up
and repot this aloe.

The Sock

I spotted in my laundry bag
someone else's sock,
which had managed to escape
its unwanted family and
adopted itself into mine
via the cavernous chasm
of the dryer.

It was a typical black,
easily paired with the
many I had, but stood out
being two sizes too big.
Inside a shoe, though,
you couldn't tell.

Two years on and here it
still is, as I
fold my warm clothes,
pair it up with a widowed sock
casually and without comment,
as if I was afraid of
hurting its feelings.

It's been a rough day and
I don't think I know

who I am anymore.
People seem to leave at
the first sign of pain
and I'm bracing for loss
all the time.

And over and over I
doubt if there's still
reason enough to fight,
but over and over the sock
turns up, and I feel
like I'm doing something right.

Uniforms

The minute I started folding my uniforms
for the last time, my imaginings took me to a
different era where I was another person.
And looking back, as anyone would say about
the past, I could not imagine how I managed
to be that person back then.

And, brushing my fingers over the white and
blue
collar, I put down my old skin and released a
breath. It had weighed a tonne and had weighed
me
down so that the ground beneath my feet kept
the imprint of my footsteps like a mark I would
leave even if I never came again.

I would not want to return, not to the treadmill
of what I began to call my life. I had seen time
wasting away before my eyes, the time I could
never
get back, the time I sold to survive. It had to
stop, or else I'd be too old, too frail, too weak
to even use my pen.

And although you might not remember who I
am
now I've chosen to be me, at least I've been that
person people thought I had to be. So no more
donning uniforms for yet another fight. Tread on
my
footprints if you will, and think of me sometime.
We always knew one day it had to end.

On the Disappearance of the Milk

It wasn't me who drank the last drop.
That would be absurd, seeing as it
wasn't even mine. It was yours, and you
finished it. That much you know is true.

But I will say this, and say it this once,
I did take a drop or two on Monday and
maybe on Wednesday too. I had a hand in it,
yes, I had a part to play in the quick
consumption of the bottle you brought home.

But have you not also taken a drop
of my soap? There are only two bottles of
washing up liquid on the sink, and
there are four of us. I'm sure I've given
you back your milk's weight in soap,
and, dare I say it, with interest.

So let us be fair. Soap cannot be drunk,
and milk cannot scrub the dishes clean.
But the one thing we needed the moment
we needed it — that is what makes
a dairy cow and a soap factory equal and
profitable in every measure.

(Unless the other soap bottle is yours,
then in that case I am very sorry.)

Not an Excuse

It could not be helped.
I've given away a book,
all for lack of space
and the prospect of moving.
I need a moment to sulk.

To Have Even Once

My clothes smell like him.
Like formula milk in fresh and vomit form,
like baby lotion and clean diapers,
like chocolate syrup on ice cream,
like soap and freshly ironed pyjamas.

My ears sound like him.
In spasms of laughter from tickles,
in echoes of crying from boredom,
in hums of soft, gentle snoring,
in whispers of almost-words.

My hands feel like him.
The soft, smooth innocence of red cheeks,
the strong, jaunty resilience of young limbs,
the wispy, delicate strands of black mane,
the hand that grips my finger.

To have even once
a memory like this,
is to have something deeper
than joy or bliss.
So I go every week
and my heart could burst —
I was one of the few
to love him first.

Corelle When It Breaks

You hear the sound, and the game is afoot.
Ten-year-olds make the best Nancy Drews.
Hide, before the evil nanny-witch sees you
lurking.
Hold your breath.

She's gone for groceries, the coast is clear.
Bring little sister along, for
every Sherlock needs a Watson.
Search the bins for evidence.
This isn't a whodunnit, we already know it was
her.

Out in the back, see there, among the rocks
and the dirt — something white, glinting in the
sun
like a corpse with its finger sticking out.
Run, see what it is.

Your mother's prized china.
Oh, if only it were anything but that.
Corelle, when it breaks, sounds like any other
broken thing.
The witch is back. Time to wrap it up.

The confrontation ensues; we've got her at last.
Tears streaming down her guilty face.
Mother knows it was an accident, but
the coverup made it a crime.

The witch glares at me.
"Are you happy now?" she screams.
And you know what,
Yes, I am.

Pyjama party tonight.

Thoughts While Hungry

A pickle was something else once,
before the immersion.
I wonder if it knows.
Would it have had
a better life as one thing
or the other?
I must ask one day
whether it's better to
go into someone's plate
as a pickled onion
or a fried one.

A poem using the word magnets on my fridge

write with a puzzle and
fix the memory

summer was grand
autumn golden
how has the winter crept in

children play in secret
can we sing silently too
must you be gone &
always far away from me

but rain will fall as spring
comes & daffodils will
still bloom after the cold night

life is beautiful
remember that

Meet Up for Coffee

I'm wrapping your present
when you ring me and ask
if you and I and everyone else
can meet up for coffee.

Is it weird that I would
go out of my way to get you
a present, but not want
to meet up for coffee?

I could save on postage
and see your face light up
as I hand you my gift
when we meet up for coffee.

But truth be told, right now
I'd rather buy stamps than a drink,
rather be doing anything else,
than meet up for coffee.

Believing in Dreams and All That

Feel the song of the ukulele
so physically close to your heart,
the notes vibrate in your chest.

G-C-E-A
Beautiful on their own, but
play them together and it's magic.

I was nine when my teacher said
to get one for ten silver coins,
just cheap enough to practise with.

My mother went to town and
got me one for a thousand coins,
something a musician could autograph.

She was trying to tell me something
about my talents and my worth
and believing in dreams and all that.

I got the message, but afterwards thought,
if I can get this on a random day,
imagine what I'll get for Christmas.

Holding Hands With Kid Gloves On

A tiny leaf landed on my shoulder after our walk
to place a comforting touch where it lay, despite
the rain.
Almost as if it heard the words we could not
bring ourselves to say.

Cover Girl

When I was sixteen, I was on the
cover of the school paper.

In my uniform, my back to the camera,
face forward, looking out of a

floor-to-ceiling window
into the horizon.

My teacher said my only problem was
proving it was me.

I thought I'd rather not,
because I looked too fat.

He was right, of course.
I know that now.

We don't need to be perfect,
we just need to be known.

Stand proud. Be in the picture.
And turn our head to the side, for crying out
loud.

Eight O'Clock

Back in the day, when I had to
be in bed by eight o'clock,
it was ten minutes before
the end of The NeverEnding Story.

I think no one told my dad
that The NeverEnding Story doesn't
actually run forever and ever.
I wish he knew that.

I wouldn't have thrown a tantrum.

And he wouldn't have had to
punish me.
And my mum wouldn't have had to
take a blow for me either.

Oh, what pains we take
for a figure of speech.

It took me over 25 years to
pick up the film and finish it.
I didn't know I needed to
finish it. Until I did.

I'm never asleep at eight.
Come get me now. I dare you.

Belated Present

24

I think I've got the dreaded virus
and just when I stopped working in a hospital.

I was there when it first struck,
saw people die who had smiled at me the day
before.

I was there in full gear, barely recognisable
as everyone else breathed through machines.

And I didn't even care about cleaning every
pen I used or washing every grape I bought.

If getting it meant I didn't have to be there
for a while, then I would love a break.

I didn't get it then.
Not when I was immersed in it.
Not when I wanted it for my escape.

Dreams

25

My dreams will never come true.
It is useless to believe that
I am a good writer
Because I eventually realise
My work isn't as brilliant as I thought
And I won't fool myself thinking
There is great work waiting to be written
Because every day is proof
That I'm better off with a job that pays the bills.
No words of advice will convince me
I can still be better at this.
Because despite what I thought,
I am rubbish at stringing words together.
And I have no reason to think
I can be awesome one day
And I know this because
What they say about dreams is a lie.

(Now read backwards.)

When Water Boils

When water boils, does it feel pain?
When it turns to steam,
does it feel loss?
When it condenses back into liquid,
does it feel restored?
Does any transition into any form
cause it discomfort of any kind?

If I could handle change like water,
I would change all the time.
Take the shape of champagne one minute,
fly with the birds the next.
Love you today and be two litres,
Lose you tomorrow and be one —
merely a matter of maths.

But would I give up my every reaction
for a life of numb calculation?

Ask me again when you go.

Talisman

I've had my hefty Bible
since I was about fifteen,
and did not want to use it
for I liked to keep it clean.

Besides, the fact I have it
ought to count to some degree.
And if I die, its presence
on my shelf will then save me.

If someone shot me in the
chest, the bullet wouldn't hit,
but go straight to the Bible
in my pocket, should it fit.

And if my plane should suddenly
have all its engines stall,
then surely by some miracle
this book would break my fall.

But later I discovered
it's no use unless I read
the words that God had written
so from death I could be freed.

It's not the book that saves me
but the name that lies therein,
I'm glad I didn't get shot or crash
before I could begin.

Writer's Block

Clocks ticking
through silent hours,
lost words and blank thoughts.
Agonising, pondering,
yet nothing hour after hour.
Paper wasted, mind numb.
Maybe tomorrow, change.
Will it?
It will
change tomorrow, maybe.
Numb mind, wasted paper.
Hour after hour, nothing yet.
Pondering, agonising,
thoughts blank and words lost,
hours silent through
ticking clocks.

The Notebook

Once, on holiday when I was eight,
my mother went to the market
in the seaside town where my
grandmother lived, and brought me
home a notebook.

The most random notebook in the
world. I can't remember if I had
asked for it, or if she thought it
would make a nice present, but she
got it for me and I loved it.

There was a picture of a child actor
on the front cover. I liked him;
I thought he was handsome. Come to
think of it now, I probably asked her
to get it because of that cover.

On the inside was lined paper that
held the evanescent promise of
great things distinct to every blank
sheet that ever lived. I sat staring
at the promise for a while.

The notebook is gone now, I'm not
sure how I lost it. And some days I
wonder if it knows the secret that it
holds. For after I stared at its pages,
I gave it my very first poems.